12 STEPS TO PUBLISHING

Workbook
by Connie Dunn

12 Steps to Publishing: Workbook by Connie Dunn, Copyright © 2014

Published by Nature Woman Wisdom Press

First Edition. Printed and bound in the United States of America.

All rights reserved. No part of this book may be reproduced in any form or by any electronic or mechanical means., including information storage and retrieval systems, recording, or photocopying, without permission in writing from the publisher, except by a reviewer, who may quote brief passages in review or where permitted by law.

Copyright © 2014 Connie Dunn
ISBN-13: 9780615968285
ISBN-10: 0615968287

Dunn, Connie

12 Steps to Publishing: Workbook

Book Writing

12 Steps to Publishing: Workbook

by Connie Dunn

Book Publishing

12 Steps to Publishing: Workbook

by Connie Dunn

Book Marketing

12 Steps to Publishing: Workbook

by Connie Dunn

Independent Publishing

12 Steps to Publishing: Workbook

by Connie Dunn

Self Publishing

12 Easy Steps to Publishing: Workbook

by Connie Dunn

STEP 1 - Get Clear on What You're Writing

Book Concepts

The best book concept is one that speaks to you. If you have a collection of poetry add pictures to make a book. Not a photographer? Collaborate with family or friends for photos. If you've been writing a blog, this could be turned into a book.

Blogs and newsletters make up a body of work that you've already created. You can use each as a chapter in your book, then expand on the topic. Or, you can just use the information you've put together to create your own, unique book.

Other Concepts Include: Inspirational or Meditational Books; Books of Quotation that include your own interpretation, action items, or questions; Silly sayings that you can add a story about how it came about or how it manifested in your life.

A good book is short. More and more people have shorter amounts of time to read. However, a short book needs to be meaty or deep in content. If you write a Blog, you can put them together, and maybe expound on them to create a book. You can do the same with your newsletter.

Action Items

List all your book concepts and pick the one that you feel the most passionate about.

_____

_____

_____

_____

Audience

Your audience is the people for whom you are writing your book. For example, a text book is written for students. A fiction book for middle-school students is written for middle school students. Blogs and newsletters are written for customers or clients. Expanding on these will help you figure out how to create a book from them.

Knowing who your readers are will help you write to their interests. This audience is your target market. When the audience is too broad, it is more difficult to identify specific target groups for whom you can market.

When the audience is more pin-pointed, you are able to reach them easily, because you'll know what they like and don't like as a group. For whom are you writing this book?

The Audience is something you need to know before you begin writing, because…You need to know how to speak to them. For example, if you were writing for 3rd grade or 12th grade, you would not use the same sentence structures. You would write differently to reach plumbers or stock brokers.

When thinking about your ideal reader, try to describe this person in as much detail as possible. Your audience might be broken into more than one group. Your TARGET audience is your primary audience. Your SECOND TARGET audience is you secondary audience. The secondary audience can be useful when marketing, so that you can add onto what you are primarily doing.

Action Items

Think about who your potential readers are. Think about your primary and secondary markets and list them below:

_____

_____

_____

_____

Your Hope for Publishing

Your DREAM of publishing is important. What role with publishing will impact your life?

Action Items

What do you hope to receive from publishing this book? Will you be proud to present a copy of your signed book to your mom or another relative? Will being a published author help you professionally by getting you noticed in your industry? Will being published bring some other quality to your life? What are Your Benefits? Write these in the blanks that follow:

_____

_____

_____

Titles

The Title of a Book is NOT Copyrightable, so you can use a title that has already been used. Titles of Books need to **Hook Readers**, especially when your reason for writing the book has to do with your profession. In fact, if your book is acting in the role of your business card, that title needs to be catchy and one that people will remember – in the right catchy manner.

Clever Titles can get notice, but be careful, it can also get noticed for the wrong reason.

While the **Title** comes at the first of your book and I have put it in **Step 1**, it does not have to be the first thing you do. You may choose this title later or find one that is a "working" title and choose a different one later.

Short Titles are best. Sub-titles can give more information about what your book is about.

Resources for Creating Titles:

Title Generator: http://www.kitt.net/php/title.php Headline Analyzer, analyzes the emotional marketing value of a headline (can be used for titles, as well): http://www.aminstitute.com/headline

According to Robert Scott Lawrence, an attorney who specializes in intellectual property and copyrights, the ten best titles are: *I killed Hemingway*; *The Roaches Have No King, God Hates Us All*; *Print the Legend*; *One Hundred Years of Solitude*; *Zen and the Art of Motorcycle Maintenance*; *Even Cowgirls Get the Blues*; *A Confederacy of Dunces*; *Ham on Rye*; *Trouble Is My Business*.

According to Robert C. Parker, these are the 10 best tips to creating good book titles: Promise a benefit; Be concise; Target your specific readers; Be specific; Position your book; Use metaphors to make your title memorable; Engage your readers interest. Use imperative or action verbs; Use Web-friendly titles; and Test your title.

To be totally fair, I thought I'd give you're the 10 most controversial titles, offered by The Shark Guys.com: *The White Man's Burden*; *White Slave*; *The Missionary Position*; *That Bitch*; *Smart Girls Marry Money*; *Why Do I Vomit? and Other Questions about Digestion*; *God Is Not Great*; *Forty Million Dollar Slaves*; *The God Delusion*; *The Trouble with Islam*; and *N*gger: The Strange Career of a Troublesome Word*.

According to James Chapman, host of *A Passion for Writing*, the 10 most read books are: *Diary of Anne Frank*; *Think and Grow Rich*; *Gone with the Wind*; *Twilight, the Saga*; *The Da Vinci*; *The Alchemist*; *Lord of the Rings*; *Harry Potter*; *Quotations from Mao Tse-Tung*; and *The Holy Bible*.

Action Items

Write down all your *Title* ideas, taking into account, who your target market is.

_____

_____

_____

_____

_____

Outline

For maximum results for your book, outline your book. Even if you choose to revise it later, outlining helps you to organize your thoughts, ideas, and other information. There are many methods of outlining, such as your old high school English style outlining with Roman Numerals and details.

Outline Example

I.   Main Topic
     a. More Details
     b. More Details
 	
II.   Next Topic
     a. More Details
     b. More Detail
 	
III.   Third Topic
     a. More Details
     b. More Details

The best way to outline a book; however, is to create the Table of Contents. Under each category, you can write a bit about what you plan to write. Addig notes about what resources you have can also be helpful.

Table of Contents
Chapter 1   This chapter is about how to begin. Chapter 2   This chapter tells the story. Chapter 3   This chapter further details the story.

Don't worry about whether you will need to change how your book flows down the line. Change happens as we write, simply make the changes that you think are essential and necessary.

If your book takes a turn you didn't anticipate, don't be concerned. You can rewrite the outline from that point on. Redoing the outline does help you stay on track

Action Items

Write an outline for your choice of book concepts. Your outline can be as simple as a your **Table of Contents** or more complicated outline that explains what you will be putting into each chapter. NOTE: If you need more pages, add them.

_____

_____

_____

_____

_____

_____

_____

(NOTE: Type the Table of Contents on your computer/tablet/laptop)

Assignments

Begin Your First Chapter (NOTE: Does not have to be Chapter 1)
NOTE: To do this most effectively, write on your computer/laptop/tablet. If you are challenged in writing on your computer, begin in a 3-ring/spiral binder or yellow legal pad.

STEP 2 – Establish Writing Habits

Must Have Techniques for First-Time Writer

Choose one project to work on. Write down notes that come to you for other books, but resist writing on them. Carry a digital recorder with you so that you can record ideas for your book.

Don't sweat the small stuff. Get your stories, information, or whatever it is that you're writing down on paper…or rather into the computer…you can fix everything else in the editing process.

There is no replacement for time writing; however, when you have writer's block, the best thing to do is do something else. You can process your story while doing other things. You just don't need to make this an excuse for not writing.

Regular Schedules

The biggest secret to writing a book is that you have to actually sit down and write it! Establishing good discipline for writing helps you maximize your writing time. Set aside one day, one morning, or one afternoon per week to write.

Naturally, if you are planning to write a book in a certain length of time, you have to adjust your writing schedule. If you have decided to write a 100 page book with an estimated completion time 30 days away, then you must write 3.333 pages per day.

Keep in mind that there is quite a bit of work beyond the actual writing. Editing and Rewriting needs to be figured into your timeline. Formatting, which includes placing any graphics into your book, also has to be figured into your timeframe

Once you are ready to upload the interior pages, which is your book manuscript, then you will need to:
- Create a Cover
- Review a Proof
- Approve your Proof
- Order some Books

There is no substitute for actual time writing. Scheduling your time needs to be realistic. If your work schedule is tight now, it is doubtful that it is going to clear up to give you the time you want to write. Therefore, you have to create that time by working it into your schedule.

The secret to scheduling realistic time into your schedule is a negotiation. What are the work goals? What are the writing goals? How can you negotiate time for both?

Negotiating with yourself sounds more complex than it really is. Look at all your time demands and prioritize them. Often, we overload our schedules with items that aren't as important to our ultimate work goals as we might ordinarily think. Carving out writing time requires that you make some sacrifices of time somewhere.

Mothers often stay up late after the children are in bed or get up very early before they are ready to rise. Some entrepreneurs that I know simply cross off time out of their schedules. It sounds simple, but sticking to a schedule is not always easy.

Get out your calendar and write down your commitment to writing.

Accountability

Creating a schedule gives you a plan in which to work: The second secret that I'd like to share with you is: Being Accountable. Being accountable indicates that someone is holding you to your schedule. Having an accountability partner that reciprocates proves to be a good choice for both parties.

On the following lines, discuss your writing goals and how you plan to stay accountable.'

Writing Styles

Developing a unique style often takes years to develop. However, there are some decisions that you can make to hurry that style along: Writing from a personal standpoint; formal writing; factual writing; or a combination of these.

My style is more personal, which includes storytelling when possible. I also write from the personal viewpoint rather than from third person, which means for fiction writers that you only know what one character is thinking.

e e cummings developed his own style of writing, where there were no capitalization and no punctuation. While it worked for him, it is difficult to read. Punctuation helps us understand what words to emphasize and where to take a break.

Developing your own style of writing begins with writing naturally or similar ways in which we talk. This is especially critical in fiction writing, because in writing phonetically, at times, we get their ethnicity just from reading their dialog.

If you've been writing a blog for a while, you may have developed a particular way of writing those, which means that you probably developed your writing style. If you are writing your book from your blogs or newsletters, pay attention to how you've written them and continue that in your book.

Common Book Writing Mistakes

A big mistake is trying to write about a topic that you don't know enough about. For example, if you are a hair stylist, but you are writing a book about building rocket ships, you are probably not writing about what you know best.

Another common mistake is making a lot of grammatical and spelling mistakes. I usually tell my writers not to look at these while writing. These mistakes are easily fixed during the editing process. I highly recommend using a professional editor for the editing process rather than your girlfriends' friend. Books with a large number of this kind of mistake screams self-published and amateur!

When we choose to publish a book, especially as an entrepreneur, we must make it the best that we can. There will always be one or two errors that get overlooked. That's normal! Publishing a book with a lot of errors is much like walking into your client's office without your pants or skirt.

Keep in mind how you are going to market this book. Do you market other flawed products? Probably not! So...get your book edited by a professional editor, or someone for whom editing is their job.

Assignments

Begin Your Second Chapter (NOTE: Does not have to be Chapter 2)
NOTE: To do this most effectively, write on your computer/laptop/tablet. If you are challenged in writing on your computer, begin in a 3-ring/spiral binder or yellow legal pad.

Step 3 - Learn Good Interviewing Skills

Interviews

If you need the most relevant industry information, you can interview industry leaders. Using an interview to gain the knowledge needed, can make your book more interesting; especially when you are capturing stories not just information. While there is a place for pure information, stories are still the best way to communicate many things.

Stories are one of the oldest forms of communication. Some of the ancient tribal communities in Africa, for example, passed on their stories through dance and songs. Think about singing your history - probably not an easy task!

Getting the appropriate information means you must think carefully about what it is you want to get from each interview. Make sure your interview collects the most relevant information by asking the right open-ended questions

Technology can help record your interviews. However, as a journalist, I found that using tape recorders (now digital recorders) and taking notes were the most effective. That way if the tape failed, I had notes.

Interviewing anyone, whether they are a CEO, President of the United States, or Joe Bloe from NoWhereInParticular, needs to be done in a professional manner, which means that you need to create some questions to ask before you do your interview.

Phone or in-person interviews are fine. In-person interviews are often difficult to schedule due to geographical differences or schedules. When possible, schedule your interview for a specific time, even if the interview will be done by phone. Be prepared for your interview by having relevant questions ready.

When creating questions to use for interviewing, make sure you ask open-ended questions. If your interviewee can answer yes or no, you won't get what you need out of the interview. For example, ask: Tell me about your experience with (open-ended) vs: Did you enjoy your time at (closed)...E-mailing questions to people can also work well to getting the information you need.

If possible, pick out more people to interview than you think you need. Some people are more talkative than others. Some you may never reach. Make sure to transcribe your notes right after your interview, so you will remember what you wrote. You may be able to just transcribe your tape, but it is always good to know as soon as possible.

Make sure to transcribe your notes right after your interview, so you will remember what you wrote. You may be able to just transcribe your tape, but it is always good to know as soon as possible.

Decide whether you need to do some interviewing for your book. Use the space below to list the people that you need to call.

Decide what questions you need to ask. Use the space below to write out your questions:

Research

Researching the most relevant material means you need to have given some thought about what it is you need. Then go to the right source!

One way to write about significant topics is to do the research to find out what those are. Even when you think you know a topic, it is good to do a bit of research to make sure you are not leaving out key issues and to see what others are saying.

Research comes high on my list of things to do when writing a book. No matter what genre, there are always things to check out. For example, if you are telling stories about a time period or geographic location, you may need to verify facts.

The best and most relevant source of industry information comes from people who work in the industry for which you are going to write. That source may be you!

If you are the source, then you may need to interview yourself to determine what it is that your readers and customers want to know. If you've been supplying this sort of information in blogs or newsletters, then writing your book may be a snap!

While research is often essential in writing a good book, it's possible that you've done this step by writing your blogs and/or newsletters. In Step 1, this was discussed as a Book Concept. Exploring what competitors write about can also be a helpful research in creating your book.

Researching of any kind can easily be done on the computer these days; however, not everything you read online is accurate. Wikipedia, for example, is written by a variety of people like you, me, and maybe even people who intentionally lie.

Good research sites online are universities, online magazines, universities studies, newspapers online, and white papers from major corporations in the industry from which you want information. Otherwise, public libraries or university libraries are good choices

If you want to make a point of some significant real event, then you need to check your facts. When writing a book, keep in mind that people rely on you to have done your research. Other people will quote your book. Eventually, the misinformation is traced to you, which damages your reputation.

If you are blatantly wrong about something, this gets attached to your name. This is especially important when you are writing a book to give yourself credentials and become an industry leader. Check your facts!

If you use dates of events that are real, even in fiction, you should always check your facts. For example, if Paul Ryan (Vice Presidential Republican Hopeful) or whoever wrote his speech had done their fact checking, he wouldn't have appeared to be a liar. He stated in a debate that an automobile manufacturing plant closed and blamed that on the current Obama Administration.

However, the plant closed two years earlier than Ryan stated, which clearly made him seem to have lied to the Nation in an effort to tarnish the competition. While with politicians it is hard to determine whether his statement was intentional or a mistake. When mistakes are in hard copy like in a book, it is difficult to make apologies

Mistakes are made in almost every book, but you do not want to be the person that made a colossal boo-boo that could have been alleviated by simply doing the research. You cannot rely on an editor to check your facts. As a writer, this is your responsibility.

Here's the rule of thumb: if you put a date on anything that is supposed to be real, you need to verify it's correct. If you put a town into your story, and the town is real, you need to make sure that you've spelled it correctly. Make sure what you say in your book that is supposed to be true actually is true by checking out your facts! You can get away with a little poetic license, but you cannot get away manufacturing truth in a non-fiction manuscript.

Because each book is different and often from chapter to chapter, as well, you need to determine what you need to research and where you will find the information. This information is in this section, but you may not know what to research at this time. However, if you do know now or can think ahead using your table of contents, use the space below to plan out what you need to research and where would be the best place to do your research: online or at the library. With more and more information being put online, it is possible to find what you want online. Just make sure that what you're looking at is from a legitimate site. When you have questions about things, you can often find the same type of information on several sites. Therefore, you have built in a safety margin.

_____

_____

_____

_____

_____

_____

_____

Proper Handling of Quotes and Plagiarism

So, once you do some research and want to put that information in your book, there is a right way to do it.

If you quote someone, you need to show who you quoted. If you are doing a bibliography, you still need to attribute who wrote or said what you are quoting in the body of your manuscript. You also need to make sure you quote someone accurately.

Over the years that I worked as a journalist, the one thing that really upset the people that I interviewed was not getting quoted accurately. They always made a point of telling me this when I set up their appointment. Therefore, I made a bigger effort in making sure that I quoted them in their words. Although I usually do correct grammatical mistakes, such as using the wrong tense or something glaringly wrong, it isn't hard to quote people if you are diligent with your note taking.

The other thing that people get upset over is the spelling of their name. I always make sure that I double check the spelling when I am quoting someone. It doesn't take long to verify the spelling of their name, and it is just good etiquette to make sure all names are spelled correctly. Remember: when your source is a person, they need to feel that their input is handled in the spirit in which they gave it.

Quotes should be inside quote (" ") marks. You can use it this way: "Billie goats can do a bit of damage," says Farmer Jones. Or: According to the office of agriculture, "Billie goats can do a bit of damage."

Longer quotes should be indented and italicized.
> *According to the book, Goddess Rituals: Reclaiming Our Ancient Spiritual Heritage: Rituals are basically things we do over and over again, such as bedtime routines parents do with their children, birthday parties, and other seasonal celebrations. This book contains archetypal information about 250 Goddesses from just about every ancient culture. This book teaches you how to use these Goddesses as archetypes for our lives, as well as how to use them in rituals.*

Make sure you don't use other's material wrongly. Quotes are fine, but if you steal other people's material and pass it off as your own, that's plagiarism. Not only are you setting yourself up to be sued, you may earn yourself a bad reputation, which will affect the rest of your writing career. And if you are writing a book to gain prestige in your career, don't create the opposite effect

Assignments

Begin Your Third Chapter (NOTE: Does not have to be Chapter 3)
NOTE: To do this most effectively, write on your computer/laptop/tablet. If you are challenged in writing on your computer, begin in a 3-ring/spiral binder or yellow legal pad.

Step 4 – What Goes in the Front Pages

Title

Bastard Title Page, Half Title Page, or Title Page is the inside Title Page. Your cover can look similar to these pages, but it is not necessary that they are exact copies of each other.

A Half Title Page contains only the title of the book and is typically the first page you see when opening the cover. This page and it's verso or the back side, which is a left-hand page are often eliminated to conserve pages. A Frontispiece is when there is an illustration on the verso facing the title page. This would mean that it is on the back side of the cover.

A Title Page simply shows the title, subtitle, author and publisher of the book. Sometimes the publisher's location (city and state) and the year of publication is shown on a Title Page. The Title Page might also contain illustration(s).

A Bastard Title Page is often the first page of a book. It is used interchangeably with Half Title. It is more accurate to describe it as a Fly Leaf or Fly Title. Its origin dates back to our first printed books more than 300 years ago. In the early days of printing, binding was done as a separate step. So a Fly Leaf or extra blank page was wrapped around the pages to keep them together. Printing on the Fly Leaf was usually kept to Title only and was followed by a Title Page. Through the years, the Bastard Title Page has been used in place of the Half Title and Title Page.

In practice, the Bastard Title became useful in early years of printing as book owners instructed their Book Binder to cut the title out of the Fly Leaf and paste it onto the spine. Today, the Bastard Title is often a term used to describe the inside Title Page. While its origin is more in sync with the Half Title Page, this term still hangs around. The dictionary shows its meaning as the first page of a book.

Currently, the Bastard Title Page may include illustrations, the title, subtitle, author names, and sometimes the name of the Publisher. It is a misnomer, of course, because that description is actually the Title Page. Bastard Title Pages are no longer needed, but the term remains. This might also be called a "Mock" Title Page. While there is quite a bit of controversy around this term, it is more often associated with the Half Title Page.

As if there wasn't enough controversy around the Bastard Title Page, there is also a Second Half Title Page. This page is used when there are a lot of pages in the front part of the book. The Second Half Title carries the title of the book

Creating a Title Page for your book is done as part of Step 1; however, if you've not done this, now would be a good time to set up a working title, even if you aren't sure about it.

Cover

The Cover is actually one of the last things that you will do.

Naturally, if you publish through a traditional publisher, you won't even need to create a cover. It seems like a good idea to discuss the cover here, because when we talk about titles, we know that a title goes on the cover.

Copyright Page

The Copyright Page generally appears on the back side of the Bastard or Inside Title page. However, it sometimes is on the backside of the Dedication Page in some books. It needs to be located in the front pages, before the first chapter and introduction.

The copyright page needs to show:
- who holds the copyright, which is you, the author
- year of the copyright
- name of publisher
- ISBN number (both the 13 digit and 10 digit numbers)
- Library of Congress Catalog Information – give every possible key words where your book could be found
- disclaimer about copying pages of your book

These are the building block for creating your copyright page.

Sample Copyright Page

Title Copyright © YEAR Author(s)
Published by XXXXXNAME of PUBLISHING COMPANY, XXXADDRESS or at least City, ST.

First Edition <Note, this would change if the book has been published before, but you've decided to release another **_Edition_** of the book.> Printed and bound in the United States of America. All rights reserved. No part of this book may be reproduced in any form or by any electronic or mechanical means, including information storage and retrieval systems, recording, or photocopying, without permission in writing from the publisher, except by a reviewer, who may quote brief passages in review or where permitted by law.

ISBN (10) <u><Note: there are two numbers here, because the 13 is the new one accommodating the growth in books world-wide; the 10 is still used by many bookstores></u>
ISBN (13)

Copyright © Year PUBLISHER(S)

Published by Production Com
Printed in The United States of America

MONTH YEAR
10 9 8 7 6 5 4 3 2 <u>*(this refers to the edition...this is edition 1, if it were the 4th edition, the numbers would start with 5.)*</u>

Library of Congress Cataloging in Publication Data

Author Last Name, Author First Name
    Title of Book
Author Last Name, Author First Name (List for Each Name of Author)
    Title of Book
Keyword Topic for Library's Card Cataloging
    Title of Book
    by Author Name and Author Name

<u>(NOTE: This page is usually done in a smaller type so that it will fit on one page)</u>

Dedication Page

The dedication page is a page where you can specifically name people or groups for whom you wrote the book. Sometimes it is also used to thank people. However, the prelude or introduction are better places for that information.

Rather than use space on the dedication page to list all the people you want to thank, it is better to put this information into your introduction or prelude.

Blank Page(s)

A blank page is normally inserted after the Dedication Page, so that whatever comes next, begins on a right-hand page. Blank pages can be inserted anywhere you need them. The left-hand page may need to be blank, in order to start a chapter on a right-hand page.

Left-hand pages are the back sides of a right-hand page.
Blank Pages don't have to remain blank. While they serve the purpose of making sure that chapters fall on the right-hand page, you can also use them to add a picture or quote. Be creative!

Foreword, Preface, Introduction

A Foreword is written by someone else, a guest. Often it is someone well-known to give your book more clout. The Foreword introduces the author to the reader.

A Preface usually tells how the book came into being, and why the book was written. This section is written by the author.

An Introduction discusses the material in the book. It should grab the reader and tell them why they should read the book. Introductions also explain how to use the book.

Table of Contents

This is fairly explanatory. You list the foreward, preface and/or introduction, as well as all the chapters with their corresponding page numbers.

Text Books and Technical Books often list headings or sub-headings in the Table of Contents; however, this is not usually done in most non-fiction and fiction books.

Indexing

Indexes do not come in the front pages, but actually go at the end. However, since they are often confused with a Table of Contents, it seemed appropriate to discuss them here rather near the end of these 12 Steps.

Indexes list all the words or terms for which you might want to find the text. For example, if this was in book form, the chapters would be the Steps that I've listed, but the bulleted items might be useful in an index. There may also be other terms that are used frequently that might also be listed in an index.

Textbooks and other non-fiction books usually sport an index. Most non-fiction books can be indexed, which adds to its usefulness. Don't get bogged down with this. You can hire the expertise to do an index for your book.

If you need help finding someone to do Indexing, contact Connie Dunn connie@publishwithconnie.com.

Assignments

Begin Your Fourth Chapter (NOTE: Does not have to be Chapter 4)
NOTE: To do this most effectively, write on your computer/laptop/tablet. If you are challenged in writing on your computer, begin in a 3-ring/spiral binder or yellow legal pad.

STEP 5 - LEARN HOW TO LEGALLY USE OTHER PEOPLE'S *MATERIAL* IN YOUR BOOK

A Quote Is a Quote

When using other people's material, you should give credit and put it in "quotes." For example:
> According to 12 Easy Steps to Publishing, "The best book concept is one that speaks to you."

Most quotes are only one to several sentences. For more information, see Step 3 on quotes and plagiarism.

Large Quoted Pieces & Copyright

If you quote large pieces from someone else's work, you need to get permission. If you don't, you are plagiarizing or stealing someone else's work. To quote large pieces, don't forget to indent and give credit. You can give credit in several ways: a footnote, a bibliography, or at the insertion point of the quote.

My preference is to give credit at the insertion point. In this way, the reader knows right away that this is a quote and from where it originates. It isn't wrong to do any of the other choices, but I prefer to do it in this way so that it is crystal clear to my reader that this is not my original information. You can also add a bibliography at the end of your book and give a list of sources from which your material came.

My preference is to give credit at the insertion point. In this way, the reader knows right away that this is a quote and from where it originates. It isn't wrong to do any of the other choices, but I prefer to do it in this way so that it is crystal clear to my reader that this is not my original information. You can also add a bibliography at the end of your book and give a list of sources from which your material came.

Pictures & Copyrights

Cover photos or graphics are generally given credit on the inside cover (Half Title or Bastard Title). Pictures that you find on the Internet should not be used, because they are protected by a common law copyright. Pictures are copyrightable. While the common law copyright will not necessarily stand up in court, you still don't want to be accused of plagiarism.

In some rare cases, you may find an old photo that is not copyrighted. This is especially prevalent when writing about historical figures. Not all old photos are copyright free. There are several ways to go about finding these historic photos. One way is to research in the archives of libraries and museums.

Internet searches may locate a source, but you probably will have to go to that source, whatever that may be. Museums often are a repository for family photos. Local museums often take in photos of the families of that area, which could be a town, city, or more regional.

In the case of museum-owned photos, they would need to give you permission to use the photos. That is usually not an issue. What becomes an issue for a museum is the removal of a photo so that it might be scanned. Take your scanner and laptop to the museum with their permission. That way the photo never leaves their premise. You need to ask permission to do so. If you want to use a picture, you should ask for permission from the person(s) who own the picture. To use a picture legally, you can find many stock pictures available on sites, such as dreamstime.com or

Poetry & Copyrights

Poetry that you find online are copyrighted or can be copyrighted. The use of someone else's poetry is plagiarism. If you find a poem that you want to use, just as in other things, you can ask permission. Most people will grant you the right to use it, depending on how you plan to use it.

Giving credit for poetry should be done at the insertion point. However, if you use a collection or series of poetry in your book, you should give credit at the insertion point to help the reader know this is not your work and clearly gives credit to whom it deserves. Also, give credit on the inside title page (same place as Cover Photo recognition).

Quotes & Copyrights

Quotes, as you have learned can be used with credit and appropriately noted. Finding quotes from Famous People on just about every topic you can imagine is an easy affair, because there are Websites set up with large databases of quotes.

NOTE: You still need to give credit for the quote. In most cases, you do not need to give a source.

If you are at a public meeting and you write down a quote from a speaker, you can quote them with credit. Of course, if you are using a large piece of what they said, make sure to indent the block quote. While anything someone says in a public meeting is available for public use, you still need to give credit the speaker and adding where the speech was given.

I often get the question: If I was watching TV, can I legally quote from this source. The answer: Yes. You must give credit for the source of your quote, which would include person and the TV news show. If this is a broadcast or rebroadcast of a public speech, you can still quote from it using the above criteria. You can quote anyone appearing on a news show if you give full credit.

If you overhear someone and choose to quote them, you could be in some hot water. Although you might give credit, you still have no right to quote what was said privately. You could get permission, of course, then you could use it.

Recipes & Copyrights

Recipes are not copyrightable as individual recipes. Recipes that are part of a published collection in a cookbook are copyrightable.

Titles & Copyrights

Titles are not copyrightable. So, if you find a title you like, you are free to use it. That's why you see titles of movies that are repeated. Titles, however, can be trademarked. This happens more frequently when the title is associated with a brand name, such as "the Pepsi generation."

Assignments

Begin Your Fifth Chapter (NOTE: Does not have to be Chapter 5)
NOTE: To do this most effectively, write on your computer/laptop/tablet. If you are challenged in writing on your computer, begin in a 3-ring/spiral binder or yellow legal pad.

Step 6 - Copyrighting Your Book

Copyrights

You do not have to formally copyright your work to prove ownership; however, it is more difficult. If you are going to prove that you are the owner of your work, you can seal it in an envelope and mail it to yourself.

You should keep the envelope unopened. The postmark will prove the date your manuscript was written. This is a viable defense if the ownership becomes contentious.

Copyrights protect intellectual property, which include books, photos, dramatic works, and other artistic works. Copyright Registration should be done through the US Government Copyright Office at the Library of Congress.

Please note that Copyright Registration can be done through a number of other private registration services. However, these services, generally, charge a fee larger than the copyright fee. Make sure you are at the US Copyright Office. You do not have to publish your work for it to be copyrighted

You should file a new copyright when a significant change is made, such as adding a new chapter. Editing changes do not count as a significant change. Copyrights protect your work, if ownership should be contested.

When to Copyright

When your work is completed, you may file for copyright registration. To file prior to completion means that you would need to re-file when the work was completed.

Your work is your intellectual property. When you have completed your work, you should copyright it with the US Copyright office.

Where to Copyright

You should file with the US Copyright Office, located in the Library of Congress.
The info for the Copyright Office is:U.S. Copyright Office, 101 Independence Ave. S.E. Washington, D.C. 20559-6000, (202) 707-3000 or 1-877-476-0778 (toll free) You can also file online at www.copyright.gov/document. html

How to File

You can file online at: www.copyright.gov. You can file by telephone by calling (202) 707-9100 to request a paper application.

You can write to: Library of Congress, Copyright Office–COPUBS, 101 Independence Avenue SE, Washington, DC 20559-6304. Request a paper application. Read all the information and follow the instructions to apply via paper application

You can write to: Library of Congress, Copyright Office–COPUBS, 101 Independence Avenue SE, Washington, DC 20559-6304. Request a paper application. Read all the information and follow the instructions to apply via paper application.

You will send back two copies of the form, your check or money order, and your document to be copyrighted. The US Copyright Office does not read your document. It is simply filed and kept in perpetuity as proof of ownership.

How to Show Copyright

Showing copyright is easy, simply use the symbol, © and the year copyrighted. Note: you can use the © even before you file. However, your document is not protected by the US Government Copyright Office until you file the forms. You will get back a form or letter stating that your document is copyrighted.

Trademark vs Copyright

A trademark is identified by this symbol: ® or ™ Trademarks indicate a brand name and include words, names, symbols, devices, or any combination.

Where a Title is not Copyrightable, it could be trademarked. Your Company Name is not Copyrightable, but it could be trademarked, as well.

For example, Coca-Cola® is a brand name and is Trademarked. Usually when you see the name, it is shown as: Coca-Cola®.

It is the USPTO.gov (United States Patent & Trademark Office) office that protects Patents and Trademarks. To learn more, go to www.uspto.gov

Assignments

Begin Your Sixth Chapter (NOTE: Does not have to be Chapter 6). NOTE: To do this most effectively, write on your computer/laptop/tablet. If you are challenged in writing on your computer, begin in a 3-ring/spiral binder or yellow legal pad.

STEP 7 - DESIGNING YOUR BOOK

Design Overview

- In this step, we will explore:
- Design Overview
- Fonts & Typography
- Profitability
- Book Trim Sizes
- Color vs Black and White
- Lay-Out Design Issues
- Picture Placement
- Picture Placement
- Creating Your Cover

You can pay someone to help you design your book, but you need to have a idea of how you want the book to look. If you don't, you may find that the book you intended to end up with doesn't exist. Not every Book Designer would take your book in a direction you wouldn't want. However, when you release your creative control, anything can happen. Be clear when you are working with people.

When designing your book, you need to take into consideration:
- Audience
- Content
- Topic
- Artistic Quality
- Personal Perspective

Audience: You need to please your audience or else your efforts are wasted.

Content: People expect good content. The books that are successful are content rich, even if they are small in page numbers.

Topic: Pick the topic that best suits your knowledge and wisdom, plus choose the perspective of that topic for your book.

Artistic Quality: Just about any book can be turned into a work of art, but some books lend themselves to it more than others. While you may think you aren't as artistic as you are good with words, remember that even words can become art.

Personal Perspective: It's YOUR book; and it's YOUR perspective! This is one of the most important REASONS that you decided to self-publish or independent publish is to have total Creative Control.

Optimizing the design of your book for readability is an important design element. Most of us know that children's picture books have large print to make it easier for beginning readers. But if your audience is the elderly, you would need to design your book with large print, as well.

Understanding your target market (Step 1) will help you better understand how the design and readability factor will affect your potential buyers. If you want to be a spend-thrift and save money by creating a book in a small point size, then you might not sell many books, because people won't purchase something they cannot read.

Fonts & Typography

Readability figures into your font style. While fancy fonts may look interesting, if you cannot read them, then people will likely not purchase the book. Notice the covers of best sellers, they usually have large san serif type.

Notice the inside of books that you are reading or go to the library on a research journey to examine the typefaces in books. Notice what you like and compare that type with available types. You can do that by making a copy of the page and comparing the type with the typeface recommended by book designers.

The inside pages are either a sans serif or serif type and normally no smaller than 12 points. If your target readers have a disability, then you must adjust to their needs.

Fonts are only part of the design, but it is a huge piece of designing a book that is both pleasing, readable, and fits the needs of your marketing niche of readers. Typography is the design of fonts. It's a bit more than most independent or self-published book designers want to think about. However, you should have a working knowledge of the topic.

Cyrus Highsmith, author of Inside Paragraphs and professor of typography at University of Rhode Island, says "When I teach letter drawing, I have observed a similar phenomena. If the students can focus on drawing the empty space inside and around the letter, 90–95% of the issues of correct proportion, balance, and weight, get resolved. Then it is just a matter of making small refinements to the letters themselves."

In Highsmith's interview posted on www.fontfeed.com, he talks about how the font is no longer a printed book design issue. The font used has to look and be readable across print, e-readers, tablets, and cell phones. That's a lot of flexibility for something most of us never think about.

Highsmith continues: "When the pages change size, columns expand or contract, as the resolution goes up and down, the typography, what goes on inside paragraphs and beyond, needs to be carefully adjusted to suit the context." That's the reason that as an independent publisher, you need to appreciate typography, even if you only know what I have added here.

The Book Designer (www.bookdesigner.com) hosted blog written by Joel Friedlander on August 31, 2009, caught my eye. Friedlander, a self-published author says, "There's no bigger decision you make in designing a book than picking the body typeface."

"Any idiosyncrasy in the type design will be magnified by the repetition of typesetting 75,000 or 100,000 words in thousands of lines on hundreds of pages," Friedlander points out. There are five basic classic fonts that are recommended by book designers that make most books look great.

Five Classic Fonts
Garamond is know for its graceful, flowing style.
Janson is set apart by its strong thick and thin strokes.
Bembo has classic beauty. It is also liked for its readability.
Caslon is the classic font used in textbooks.
Electra has warm personality.

Profitability

In designing your book for profitability, you want to keep the page number count down. At the same time, you need to make it readable. There are ways to cut your costs, such as making the interior black and white rather than color, when the color aspect doesn't matter to the overall design.

Profitability, however, must be weighed with the overall salability as a product. If you are just cutting things out of your book to save money, you may find that you are just being too thrifty. Check out the book calculator on CreateSpace to see exactly how your choices fit into the cost of the book.
https://www.createspace.com/Products/Book/#content6

Where can you save in your design? The profitability of your book depends on the quality content of your book. If you've chosen a hardback book over a paperback, then you can probably save by creating your book as a paperback. NOTE: CreateSpace.com does not offer hardback books. Lulu.com does provide that as an option.

Perhaps you wanted elaborate paintings or graphics to go into your book, but the cost up-front is enormous. Be creative and choose another artist, which might be more affordable. One way to find a reasonable artist is to go to local high school or technical school and hire a student. Rather than eliminate the graphics all together, you might look through similar designs from a stock photo distributor, such as istockphoto.com and dreamstime.com.

Rather than eliminate the graphics all together, you might look through similar designs from a stock photo distributor, such as istockphoto.com or dreamstime.com. Choose a slightly larger trim size to cut down on the number of pages.

Book Trim Sizes

Books come is some standard "trim" sizes. Trim refers to exactly what it says, trim! After a book is printed and bound, it often needs to be "trimmed" to the right size.

Some standard trim sizes are:
- 5-inches by 8-inches
- 6-inches by 9-inches
- 7-inches by 10-inches

Color vs Black and White

Your interior can be full color or black & white. The black & white version will be less expensive; however, if you have a lot of pictures, you probably will want color. There are some reasons to choose black & white, even if your graphics are color. If you want to give the feel of older times, use black & white photos or color photos but choose black & white.

If you don't have colored graphics in the interior of you book, naturally, you should choose black & white.

Laying Out Design Issues

In the olden days, which is only a few years ago, you would have to paste the text on your pages after they had been typeset. Pictures were also processed before being pasted onto your pages. In those days, you had everything separate and a blank canvass, so to speak, to fill.

You could visually see the page. The text and pictures had hot wax on the back, so you could just pick them up and then change it around, if you didn't like it. Now, everything is done inside the computer in your word processing software. If you want a border around each of your pages, you need to do that within the software.

If you want pictures to face a certain page, such as an illustration for a chapter, you need to format the pages in your word processing software to do that. Your act of formatting is what creates your Design within your word processing software. Formatting is actually the word we use for the actions of placing graphics, choosing fonts, paragraph breaks, etc. on the pages where you want them.

Once you have chosen the size of your finished book, which is called, Trim Size, set a custom page size in your word processing software, which will automatically size the pages throughout your file.

The most used size is 6-inch by 9-inch, which means 6-inches wide and 9-inches tall. Set a custom page size in your word processing software, which will automatically size the pages throughout your file.

Once the trim size is set, then you have to go through each page and make sure everything is set the way you want it. Odd numbered pages are Right-Handed Pages, which is where we typically want Chapters to begin. Even numbered pages are the back sides or Left-Handed Pages. Placing a picture on the facing page or Left-Hand Page can be a good design option.

Blank Pages need to be inserted to assure that Chapters begin on Right-Hand (odd numbered) Pages. Once you have the Page Size chosen, I usually go into the View tab and set it to 2 pages. It will show you the Right-Hand Page and its back side or Left-Hand Page. In this way, I can easily format the page breaks or pagination

You can set the page up at the very start of your writing if you know what size you want your book to be. However, formatting will still need to be done after your writing is completed and all the editing has been done. Formatting page breaks will put the pagination in order. Books have page numbers, as well. While there are a number of ways to format these, there are some standard ways that books are done.

Blank Pages need to be inserted to assure that Chapters begin on Right-Hand (odd numbered) Pages. Once you have the Page Size chosen, I usually go into the View tab and set it to 2 pages. It will show you the Right-Hand Page and its back side or Left-Hand Page. In this way, I can easily format the page breaks or pagination.

You can set the page up at the very start of your writing if you know what size you want your book to be. However, formatting will still need to be done after your writing is completed and all the editing has been done. Formatting page breaks will put the pagination in order.

Books have page numbers, as well. While there are a number of ways to format these, there are some standard ways that books are done.

Page numbers and the Book Title are often placed in the margin above (header) or below (footer) the text. One way is to put the page numbers on the outside edges of the pages, this means that odd and even pages need to be formatted differently. NOTE: Microsoft Word (2010) makes it more difficult to make this work – not impossible but difficult.

Page numbers can be centered on the page in either the header or the footer. You can center both the number and the title by putting the title in the header and the number in the footer. The page numbers and title are normally in a smaller font and are often italicized

Assignments

Begin Your Seventh Chapter (NOTE: Does not have to be Chapter 7)
NOTE: To do this most effectively, write on your computer/laptop/tablet. If you are challenged in writing on your computer, begin in a 3-ring/spiral binder or yellow legal pad.

Step 8 - Finishing Your Book

Add Massive Credibility to Your Book

- Editing
- Formatting

Add Massive Credibility to Your Book

Have someone prestigious write a Forward for you book.
In Step 4, you learned that a Foreword is written by someone other than yourself.

When thinking of someone to write a Foreword for you, think about people who are well-known in the industry for which your book is written. For example, if you are writing about technology, you might want someone like Bill Gates of Microsoft™ or Mark Zuckerberg of Facebook. You may know someone close to you that pulls some weight in your industry.

Who do you know that is someone noteworthy on the topic for which you are writing? Use the lines below to write down their names. Then do the research to find contact information. Authors can usually be reached through their publishers, if the publisher's address, etc. is listed. Otherwise, search the title and author together.

_____

_____

_____

_____

Editing

Editing is the process of reading, rewriting, compressing your sentences, and correcting misspellings, and other grammatical errors.

You should do some editing of your work, so that you can get your manuscript as clean and crisp as possible. However, professional editors can help you improve your writing, as well as, find all your mistakes that you might not see.

Formatting

Formatting is a necessary part of finishing your book, especially, for self-publishers. Once your manuscript has been edited to your satisfaction, you are ready to format. (See Step 7 for more information about editing in the final stages of Designing your book.)

Some people do the formatting as they write, if you haven't done that, this is when you do it! Start by setting the page size, which is the trim size that you have chosen from your online on-demand printer. In most word-processors, you need to choose a custom size.

If you want pictures to fall on left-hand pages, you need to format the pages so that it happens. Your inside pages, begin with your (right-hand page) Half Title or Bastard Title Page, which may have your cover picture, title, subtitle, and authors or just the title, subtitle and authors.

Starting at the Inside Title Page (Half Title or Bastard Title), make sure all the type on this page fits and is formatted to the appropriate font and size that you want. Even if you did some formatting during your writing process, you should go back through the pages again.

On the back side of the Inside Title Page is the Copyright Page, so the Inside Title is a Right-Hand Page followed by the backside or Left-Hand Page. Make sure you've put in your ISBN on the Copyright Page. The type on this face is usually smaller, which makes it easier to fit in everything you need on this page.

Formatting the Copyright Page

Formatting on the **Copyright Page** should start with the Title; Subtitle and followed with the copyright symbol (@) and your name. This should be your name, even if you've written the book with a pseudonym.

The next line should read: Published by Name of Publishing Company, which will be CreateSpace, if you don't choose a custom "Imprint." Of course, you might have chosen a different on demand printer, so that name should go in that spot. Next: First Edition. Printed and bound in the United States of America.

Next comes your disclaimer, which is very important. Wording should be similar to:

> All rights reserved. No part of this course may be reproduced in any form or by any electronic or mechanical means, including information storage and retrieval systems, recording, or photocopying, without permission in writing from the publisher, except by a reviewer, who may quote brief passages in review or where permitted by law.

Next is often the copyright repeated, followed by the ISBN. There have been two numbers given to you by R.R. Bowker, the company that assign the International Standard Book Number: one is the 10-digit old formula; second is the new 13-digit code. While the 13-digit is preferred, some booksellers prefer the old 10-git. Therefore, I include both.

What follows is a repeat of the published by and printed in the United States. While the items repeated can be eliminated due to space, the other items on the page are needed.

The two last things on this page are: Library of Congress Cataloging in Publication Data; and catalog listings. These catalog listings are what you would be cataloged under at any library. For example:

Dunn, Connie
    12 Easy Steps to Publishing
          or
Publishing
    12 Easy Steps to Publishing
    by Connie Dunn

The catalog information is important, because the libraries use this for setting up their card catalog (electronically now). If you don't give them every category that you feel the book should be found under, then it probably won't be there. So, leave out duplicate
information, make the type smaller, and add every category you can legitimately use to categorize your book.

The next page after the copyright page is a right-hand page or odd number page. This should be your Dedication page. Normally, the type is centered on this page. You may use "for" plus names or categories of people, such as writers, children, etc. You may also shrink the size on this type, if you need to do so to get it all to fit on one page.

The page that follows the Dedication Page is generally blank. You may fill it with a picture or a quote or something else that seems fitting. The next page is usually your Table of Contents, followed by your Introduction and the Chapters in your book.

Go through one page at a time, making sure each page is how you want it. Headlines should be bigger than your normal text. Make sure all the text is formatted in the appropriate font and size. Make sure pages break in the appropriate places.

You may need to put in a blank page to make the pagination work. Again, you can add a picture, a quote, or leave it blank. Blank Pages should fall on a left-hand page.

Page Numbers

Page numbers should be formatted to fall either in the center or on the edges. Usually, you put the page numbers on the outside edges. On left-hand pages, the page number should fall on the left-hand edge. On right-hand pages, the page number should fall on the right-hand edge.

Some books also add the Book Title in the header or footer. This is a style or book design decision. While there seems to be some more popular ways of designing the page numbers, there is not a hard and fast rule. Look through other published books and see what you like, then copy that style.

Assignments

Begin Your Eighth Chapter (NOTE: Does not have to be Chapter 8)
NOTE: To do this most effectively, write on your computer/laptop/tablet. If you are challenged in writing on your computer, begin in a 3-ring/spiral binder or yellow legal pad.

Step 9 - Find Your Publishing Mode

Finding Your Publishing Mode

It depends on what your goals are for publishing. Traditional to Indie Publishing are available, but some are more difficult than others.

Traditional Publishers may take up to two years to publish your book after they've accepted the manuscript. Getting the manuscript accepted is always a gamble! This is not an easy choice. You can collect hundreds of reject letters, which means you have to submit your manuscript to many of places.

The most economical and easy choice for publishing your book is Self-Publishing or Indie-Publishing, these terms are mostly interchangeable. You can publish with little to no up-front costs.

- With no budget at all, you can publish your book through CreateSpace.com, using CreateSpace Independent Publishing as your publisher.
- The book is automatically listed on Amazon.com.
- You will be given an e-store where people can buy your book.
- You can use a cover template to create your book's cover. You don't have to stock your books.
- People order and their order is filled and mailed without you having to do anything.

If costs are not an issue, then you have a lot of options. With deep pockets and a desire to publish just what you want and when you want, you can easily self-publish or indie publish. Through CreateSpace.com and some other indie publishers and online print shops, you can get all the services that a traditional publisher offers. CreateSpace.com charges about $4,634 (depending on size of manuscript) for all their services.

For the more than $4,500, you receive a variety of services, which include: basic and comprehensive copyediting, signature cover design, custom-designed book designed interior, video trailer, making your book available to libraries nationwide, book review from Kirkus Indie Review, ISBN, & online distribution.

My Recommendations

Somewhere in between is what I usually recommend to authors. While CreateSpace.com is a great name for an on-demand printer, it doesn't have a great ring as a publisher. Choosing your own imprint for your book only costs $10 per title through CreateSpace.com for the ISBN.

If you want to choose a publishing imprint that isn't your business, there are choices for that, as well. They do come with a cost, of course .I also recommend to my writers to invest in the expanded distribution, which currently is only $25 on CreateSpace.com. Other on-demand printers have other costs.

Publishing Options

- Agents (Traditional & Indie Publishers)
- Publishing Houses
- Self-Publishing
- Indie Publishing

Agents

These are the folks that help writers get into the Publishing Houses or Traditional Publishers. Agents also help authors get published with Indie Publishers; however, most Indie (Small) Publishers would talk to an author directly. NOTE: Many Indie Publisher are Self-Publishers.

These are the folks that help writers get into the Publishing Houses or Traditional Publishers. Agents also help authors get published with Indie Publishers; however, most Indie (Small) Publishers would talk to an author directly. NOTE: Many Indie Publisher are Self-Publishers.

Good Agents take on clients and their writing careers, since your success as a writer, guarantees their success, as well. Agents, however, are not your friend and not your business manager. Their job is to get you into a Publisher. They are motivated by the percentage of your royalties they will receive.

If you need money managed, hire a business manager. Friends, on the other hand, should not be hired. Fans cannot be bought either, but one needs both friends and fans to be a successful writer.

Publishing Options

Publishers offer writers an advance against future sales and a royalty to be paid after the sales exceed the advance money. The amount of the advance may only be $1,000.

Publishing Houses

Publishing companies, such as Prentice Hall, Random House, and Harper Collins, publish books that end up in book stores across the country and sometimes in various countries. These books also are on Amazon.com.

Keep in mind, although the distribution can be very wide, publishing companies often do not always distribute unknown authors in as wide an array. As an unknown author, it is difficult – not impossible – to get your book accepted by a traditional publishing house.

J.K. Rowling, author of the Harry Potter series, had an agent who submitted her work to 12 publishers. She received 12 reject letters. She was finally published by Bloomsbury in the United States.

Regional publishers often publish books created about or in their region. These publishers tend to be smaller and often fall into the Indie category, which makes them more reachable for unknown authors.

Self-Publishing

Now, in the era of electronic books and other publications, self-publishing is not only acceptable but preferable, especially for entrepreneurs for whom writing a book can be the difference of being in a field and being at the top of a field.

Not very long ago, being self-published was synonymous with not being good enough to get published by a "real" publisher. But those days are gone and so is the stigma surrounding self-publishing. With technology advancing, not only new ways of viewing books has advanced but methods of printing have gone from hot type to cold type to on-demand printing.

Self-Publishing through an on-demand printer speeds up the time from your finished manuscript to your printed book. On-demand printers are available online. Uploading a .pdf to an on-demand printer can have you planning your book launch party quickly – sometimes in less than two weeks from completing the printing process.

Indie Publishing

Indie Publishing is independent publishing, which includes all small publishers, as well as self-publishers. For those who still subscribe to the old adage that people who publish themselves are somehow less of a writer, perhaps the new term, Indie publishing, makes a difference.

According to AAP (American Association of Publishers), e-book sales are on the rise. In the Brave New World of Publishing, e-book sales acrued $1.97 billion in 2011, which was an increase over the 2010 of $838 million. The 2012 figures for the first two months were $364 million, which should result in a large increase over 2011.
A lot of the increase in e-books is attributed to more e-readers and tablets on the market, as well as, the emergence of a digital children's market.

In the Brave New World of Publishing, e-book sales accrued $1.97 billion in 2011, which was an increase over the 2010 of $838 million. 1.0

The 2012 figures for the first two months were $364 million, which should result in a large increase over 2011.

A lot of the increase in e-books is attributed to more e-readers and tablets on the market, as well as, the emergence of a digital children's market.

Assignments

Begin Your Ninth Chapter (NOTE: Does not have to be Chapter 9)
NOTE: To do this most effectively, write on your computer/laptop/tablet. If you are challenged in writing on your computer, begin in a 3-ring/spiral binder or yellow legal pad.

Step 10 - Creating Your Book Marketing Plan

This step covers Book Marketing, Marketing Plan, OnlineMarketing, and Press Packets. This step might be the most important step other than writing your book.

Marketing

In Step 1, you decided who your audience was going to be. Go back in your workbook and see what your wrote. You might refine it now that you've been writing on your book for awhile. You need to consider your target market even while you are writing. Knowing who you are writing for may help you make some writing and structure decisions. But knowing your target is essential to creating your Marketing Plan.

At this point, you may still be writing on your book. However, now is a great time to be developing your marketing plan. You need to create this plan and begin the process even before your book is finished. You must market your book just like you would your business! In fact, you need to be marketing yourself as an author.

If you are writing a book that you hope will be published by a traditional publisher, your information about the demographic market for which your book is targeted, might sway a publisher to take on your book. And at the very least, it will be needed on your book proposal to an editor.

If you're planning to Indie (self) Publish, you'll need to know your market. You will actually need to put together a marketing plan for your book. Books don't sell themselves! You will need to market them to the people who need your book. Think of the benefits someone your target readers will derive from reading your book.

Marketing Plan

A marketing plan, like your business plan starts with demographics. Who is your target market? How do you reach that target market? What blogs will your market be reading…and why?

Website

Build a Website for your book – using the benefits of reading your book. If this is a Children's Book, think about adding some interesting games or crafts centered around the book to your Website. Make sure you have information about yourself and why you chose to the write this book

You need to make sure your Website has a call to action. In other words, you need to lead them into buying your book. Brochures and Sales Pages have two different feels. However, if you can create both, you are ahead of the game. Brochures tend to be more informative about your book and you. Sales pages tend to have a marketing message – what are the benefits.

Facebook – Fan Page

Build a Facebook Fan Page for your book. Information about the book (benefits) can go into the profile.Invite people to LIKE your Fan Page. Start with your friends & family. But search out the FANS of your book! Create a video for the book and put it out on youtube.com refer people to your Website and your Fan Page.

Decide where or how you are going to market your book. If you are planning to sell your book primarily online, then you will need:
- Search Engine Optimization (SEO).
- A Blog on the topic of your book.
- Also start an e-mail list for your book.

Online

Videos that highlight what the benefits are of your book can be done simply by creating a PowerPoint Presentation and adding the voice. There are other ways, of course. Develop some Websites around the keywords you've researched.

Begin a blog so that you can continue the dialogue from your book. For example, for a non-fiction book, you could just keep adding more information about the topic of your book. If you are writing fiction, your blog might highlight some new adventures for your main character. The idea is to bring in your fans.

Design a Virtual Blog Tour

There are perhaps thousands of bloggers and some of those will likely be blogging about the topic of your book. You can ask to be a Guest Blogger. Schedule your blog tour as a launch for your book. So, if you haven't yet published your book, this will be another one of those things to do once you've finished the writing process. The idea is that you schedule your blog tour for one to three weeks - usually, daily for one week and maybe only three per week for three weeks.

There are people who will organize a blog tour for you. Naturally, all book marketing will take some time and probably money. There are several types of tours. For example, Guest Blog Tours, which means you appear as a guest writer.
Review Tours, which means getting your book reviewed on review blogs and in newsletters, magazines, and newspapers (anywhere that is appropriate for the topic of

your book). It generally works the same as a blog tour only instead of being a guest blogger, you are hoping to get your book reviewed.

Press Packet

A Press Packet is usually a folder with information about the author, a photo of your, a copy of the book cover, a synopsis of your book, and a marketing sheet showing all the benefits of your book.

About the Author

You need to have a good bio (benefit driven), and a photo. Information about the Book, including a short blurb or synopsis of the book, Testimonials & Reviews, and a photo of book cover.

Information about the Publisher

If you are self-publishing, what publisher do you show on your copyright page? This is the publisher for which you need to create information about. If the publisher is your company, don't just give information about your company. Think about whether there are other books that you want to publish and what your publishing department is going to be. Then, you are ready to write about your publishing company.

Write up information on the publishing department of your business! A brochure, a list of future publications, and other information could also go into your press packet.

Marketing Plan Worksheets

Describe your target audience by explaining in detail your ideal book purchaser.

_____
_____
_____
_____
_____
_____

What are the topics that your target audience will be interested in and how does that relate to the topic of your book. *For example, you may have written a book on starting a vegetable garden from seeds. Your target audience will be vegetable gardening and starting plants from seeds. However, other topics related to vegetable gardening, such as organic remedies for gardening plants, designing above ground gardens, patio vegetable gardens, etc.*

_____
_____
_____
_____
_____
_____
_____
_____
_____
_____
_____

Creating Your Webpage: Use the space below to work on your marketing message for your book, you might start by listing all the benefits for the reader – what will they learn, what secret are you telling them. For fiction writers, what are your characters dealing with that your audience can identify with, how can they use the story in your book to relate to their own life. For Children's Writers, design a site that is interactive in some way. If you are able to set up a school tour, even regionally, make sure you have that on your Website or in your blog.

_____

_____

_____

_____

_____

_____

_____

Design your Facebook Fan Page. Using the space below, think of all the pictures and copy that you want to put on your Fan Page. You might also think about how to get people to come *like* your page.

_____

_____

_____

_____

_____

_____

_____

_____

There are other online opportunities to market. One way people get noticed is to create a short video and upload it to YouTube. Use the space below to write out what you intend to do. Your video can be copy with voice over. Naturally, if you can make another sort of video to promote you book, then go for it!

_____
_____
_____
_____
_____
_____
_____
_____

Creating a Blog is another online way to engage readers with new content on a consistent basis. Obviously, if you've written a fictional piece, you will need to expand out of the fiction and into reality, grabbing a topic from your fictional book. Unless, you're planning a sequel, of course, then you might drop some tantalizing bits in your blog about what you have your main character doing. Get creative! For children's writers, a blog should be interactive in some way.

_____
_____
_____
_____
_____
_____

Designing a Virtual Blog. This can be quite fun or it can get tedious. Let's take this step-by-step.

First, locate some blogs for which you'd like to be a guest blogger, list them below along with contact information

_____

_____

_____

_____

_____

To get prepared for your tour, you will need to do several things. Contact the blog owner and inquire about being a guest. Schedule a time to be the guest blogger, and…you will need to have written appropriate blogs to go on each of the various blogs. As a rule of thumb, try to schedule 10 for 10 days or 3 per week for 3 weeks. You can actually do guest blogging on a longer-term basis, but concentrate your guest blogging as your launch and write about your virtual blog tour on your Website and your Facebook Fan Page.

Use the space below to write down your thoughts and ideas about your guest blogs.

_____

_____

_____

_____

_____

_____

_____

_____

Below, find another form for use in organizing your blog tour. You can print one of these pages for each guest blog or copy it into your word processing software.

BLOG TOUR Date:	Web Address of Blog
Notes for Guest Blog	**Resources, Pictures, & Misc.**

Getting your book reviewed is another activity that you need to organize. First, you need to do some research and see who is reviewing your type of book. Look in newspapers, magazines, and industry-specific publications, as appropriate. Also, research to find bloggers who are reviewing books on your book's topic. Setting up your Virtual Book Review Tour is not as easy as the Blog Tour, because Reviewers have more books than space for Review. Use the space below to record your Reviewer Information.

_____
_____
_____
_____
_____
_____
_____
_____
_____
_____

To help organize your Virtual Review Tour, I've modified the form on the previous page for your use.

REVIEW TOUR Date of Contact:	Web Address of Blog Review
Notes for Review Tour	**E-Mail Address of Editor for Book Review of Newspaper, Magazine, etc.**
	Mailing Address:
	Phone #
	Press Packet E-Mailed on:
	Press Packed E-Mailed to:
	Press Packet Mailed with Review Book on:
	Review Book Only Mailed on:
	Misc. Info.

With each Book Review, you will need to send a Press Packet. Often, you can e-mail these in advance of sending the book. Check to see how they would best like the information. Sometimes, especially where books are selected and sent out to freelance reviewers, they prefer hard copies. The form above will help you keep track of these.

A Press Packet will need to be created, see above for the individual pieces to put into your Press Packet. Have a professional photo taken to use inside your book with your bio. Then, have copies made on photo paper for your portfolio. These should be 8" by 10" photos. Often, your photographer can give you good advice on where to get copies made. There are mail order places if you need a large number, but even copy shops will make these copies for you.

Assignments

Begin Your Tenth Chapter (NOTE: Does not have to be Chapter 10)
NOTE: To do this most effectively, write on your computer/laptop/tablet. If you are challenged in writing on your computer, begin in a 3-ring/spiral binder or yellow legal pad.

Step 11 - Promotional Quotes and Other Ideas

Asking Friends and Family

Because your book may not be ready to publish when you discover you need a good quote for the back of the book, it is good to rely on friends and family. You can get them to read your raw copy and give you a quote. Because they are your friends, they are more prone to give you a positive quote.

When asking family members for a quote, ask one that does not share the same last name as yours. Make sure to emphasize to your friend or family that the manuscript is not completely ready for printing.

Give your manuscript to your friends and family while it is being edited, that way you're making the best timeline that is possible. When asking for this quote, ask them to give you the benefit that they feel appropriate. Your quotes need to have benefits, that will aid your marketing efforts.

Professional Quotes – Reviewers

Reviewers or Book Reviewers will often read your proof version. You may use her or his quotes for which you may take from the review published in their publication – newspaper, magazine, online, and more! Make sure you give credit and handle the review appropriately.

You can also pay for a review. While this is a rather new thing that reviewers will do…and only some will offer that, I would procede cautiously. More bloggers that review books are willing to do this.

Some reviewers are staff members of the publication, but more are not!

Reviewers often receive hundreds of books for each review column that they write. Because they get so many books, they cannot review each book they receive. Often, it is the Newspaper or Magazine that receives the review copies and hand-picks them for the particular reviewers. Some reviewers are staff members of the publication, but more are not!

You can find Reviewers by looking through your local and regional newspapers for book reviews. Notice what types of books that each Reviewer writes about. If similar books to your book are reviewed, then there's a good chance he or she will review yours.

For example, some reviewers only review books written by local authors. If you send them your book and you are an author from outside that area, they will not review your book. It's also a good idea to know how a publication works. Many reviewers don't pick their own books, the editor does. If this is the case and you send the reviewer your book, the reviewer cannot review the book.

If the editor of the section is the person in which the book should be directed, you need to make sure you get it to that person. If you cannot tell, send the editor a message or call him or her. Remember, you cannot rely on Reviewers for quotes for the back of your book. It is not a guarantee your book will be reviewed, even if you follow all the rules for a publication.

If the editor of the section is the person in which the book should be directed, you need to make sure you get it to that person. If you cannot tell, send the editor a message or call him or her. Remember, you cannot rely on Reviewers for quotes for the back of your book. It is not a guarantee your book will be reviewed, even if you follow all the rules for a publication.

How to Use Your Book to Get More Business for Years to Come.

Naturally, it depends on what your business is and what your book is about.
Your book can be used like a business card in some incidents. For example, when you are attending an event where your potential clients will be, your book can speak volumes for you.

Make your book a .pdf that you offer free on your Website or for signing up for your e-list. Create an e-book for Kindle and Nook. And then, still sell the book, as well. You'd be surprised how many will buy a book that they could get for free.

Give your book to anyone who might be a potential client, even if the book tells them how to do everything themselves. Use the book to get speaking engagements. Use the book to gain opportunities to teach about your expertise.

Assignments

Begin Your Eleventh Chapter (NOTE: Does not have to be Chapter 11)
NOTE: To do this most effectively, write on your computer/laptop/tablet. If you are challenged in writing on your computer, begin in a 3-ring/spiral binder or yellow legal pad.

Step 12 - Learn to Publish Your Book

Book Publishing

There are a lot of ways to publish your book. However, Indie- or Self-publishing is the easiest and fastest way to get you from a completed manuscript to a printed book in your hand. If you wish to try Traditional Publishing Methods, then go back to Step 9.

Create an Account

I have done a price comparison (Oct. 2012) and found that Lulu.com and other on-demand printers are higher in price. While they offer slightly different choices, a comparison of the same type book, length, and color, I found that Lulu.com was $8; whereas, CreateSpace.com was $3.50 for exactly the same book, which makes, Lulu about 56% more than CreateSpace. Keep comparing the choices, because over the last couple of years, I've seen a lot of change in pricing.

Lulu, however, offers choices for publishing your book that CreateSpace does not. For example, if you want a book in a landscape mode, Lulu offers that and CreateSpace does not. If you want a hardback book, Lulu offers that and CreateSpace does not. One of the big perks of CreateSpace.com and Lulu.com is that you immediately get your book listed on Amazon.com.

Step-by Step for Create Space

You need to know: Title, Author(s) Names, Page Count, and Trim Size, as well as some information about your book, which should be a teaser to draw in people to purchase your book – think BENEFITS.

After signing up for the account, you are ready to: Add a New Title. To do this, go to your Member Account and click "Add New Title." Fill in the information required about your book. If you don't have all of the information about your book, you can go back and give this information.

From the Project Home, choose ISBN. There is no charge for acquiring an ISBN through CreateSpace. However, if you wish to begin your own "imprint" or your own publishing name, there is a small charge. There is no choice with Lulu, but to choose their ISBN, unless you go to R.R. Bowker and secure your own ISBN.

Companies and Entrepreneurs often want to expand their brand through creating products, including books. Using your brand or company name, you can choose a custom ISBN. You will register this "imprint" name with
Bowker Identification Service through CreateSpace. You will use this same "imprint" for future books, so make sure you save the information.

From the Project Homepage, choose Interior File. You will need to figure out what Trim Size that you want for your book. Trim Size refers to the physical size of your book, such as 6-inches by 9-inches or a 6 X 9. Before you can figure the number of pages, you need to choose a Trim Size. Normally, the smaller the Trim Size the more pages you will have.

Formatting for the Trim Size can be done by going into your Word Processing Software and changing the page size, which will likely be a custom page size. Once you have done that, you can begin formatting the book. When you are formatting, you are creating exactly what your book is going to look like.

Do not put two spaces between sentences.

Make all your Chapters begin on a Right-Hand Page, which means that they should fall on odd numbered pages.

If you want pictures to be on a facing page, which would be the Left-Hand Page, then they need to go on even numbered pages. Sometimes, this means you must enter a blank page.

Chapters should fall on odd or Right-Hand Pages. You might also refer to Left-Hand Pages as the Back Side of a Right-Hand page. Entering Hard Page Breaks, you can format the pages to land on appropriate pages. Again, when you are formatting, you are creating exactly what your book is going to look like.

To make the formatting and pagination easier, you might be able to use a template to help. CreateSpace does offer a Template for Microsoft Word® that can help.

To make the pagination go faster, I often reduce the pages to show two pages at once. It shows a left-hand and right-hand page or the back of the previous page and its facing right-hand page. You also need to verify that you have entered your ISBN into the appropriate place in your manuscript.

After you have finished formatting your book, you are ready to upload your book's Interior Files. To do this, log into your Member Account; click on the appropriate Book Title, which will take you to the Project Homepage. In the Setup Menu, click on Interior, then upload your book.

This takes you to a page that allows you to choose Trim Size or the finished size of your book; black and white or color (choose color, if you have color photos in the interior pages). If you have a question, look for A Step-By-Step Guide to Formatting Your Book's Interior on the CreateSpace Project Homepage for more help. Also, if you have difficulties that you cannot resolve, CreateSpace has a good help desk.

Once you have uploaded your Interior files, you can go to the Cover (to be truthful, you can go to the Cover prior to uploading your Interior files, but you cannot Submit the

Cover until the Interior is uploaded). Once you are on the Cover Page, click on the Build Your Cover Online choice and then click on the Launch Cover Creator. On this page, you can add the information on the left-hand side that is requested. There is also an option of creating your own cover and uploading it. Look for a template, which makes this easier.

In the middle of the page will be choices for your cover, these are the templates. Note that font or typeface can be changed using the built-in choices. Background colors and font colors can be changed to a wide variety of colors. You can keep changing the templates until you are happy with it. If you don't like it, you can upload a different template. All the information and cover graphic is retained and added to the new template.

Submit your Cover!

Complete Setup by choosing this from the Project Homepage. During this step, you will be finalizing your book. There is a review process, then you can choose a hard copy proof to buy or do an online proof approval.

Next, you will go to the Distribution choice on the Left-Hand Menu on the Project Homepage. There are several steps to Distribution. The FREE Choices includes Amazon.com, Amazon-Europe, and CreateSpace E-store.

I recommend also choosing the Expanded Distribution, which offers you the opportunity to access a larger audience through more "online retailers, bookstores, libraries, academic institutions, and distributors within the United States. NOTE: Some of these Expanded Distribution options are not available if you have chosen your own Imprint and Custom ISBN. However, you are still put into Ingraham Distribution, which puts your book on the purchase list for a wide variety of book sellers.

While the Distribution opportunity is widened, this choice Expanded Distribution will also improve your book costs. Lowering your cost is ultimately your goal. While lowering the cost per book, you want the highest quality, as possible, so that you can set the price per book at a reasonable price. Of course, you want to make money, as well, so it's a balancing act.

Let me give you an example: If your book cost is $3.50, you could sell your book for $10 and your profit would be $6.50. The $3.50 would be your cost when you order copies of your own book. There is some thought in the world of marketing that setting your price a penny less: $9.99 makes it more appealing to the public. You could even sell this book for $10.99 or even $14.99, if you want to make more. You need to weigh in the making money with affordability. Also, you make less when other bookstores, including Amazon, sell your book. On the other hand, you sold a book, which is better than not selling it!

Another issue in setting price is to understand what the market will bear. For example, a book selling for $9.99 can be considered too cheap; therefore, an inferior product. Or, $14.99 makes it more appealing, because this price says that the product must be a superior product.

Your book goes on Amazon.com immediately after you approve your book after reviewing online or through a proof. On Amazon, you are in front of millions of potential buyers.

Your last task: Order Books!

Assignments

Begin Your Twelve Chapter (NOTE: Does not have to be Chapter 12)
NOTE: To do this most effectively, write on your computer/laptop/tablet. If you are challenged in writing on your computer, begin in a 3-ring/spiral binder or yellow legal pad.

At this point, you should have you book either finished or nearly finished. You will have learned a lot about self-publishing or indie-publishing.

Thank you for participating in this course!

www.ingramcontent.com/pod-product-compliance
Lightning Source LLC
Chambersburg PA
CBHW060327240426
43665CB00047B/2807